The ABCs to Student Success

HAYLEY MULENDA

authorHOUSE®

AuthorHouse™ UK
1663 Liberty Drive
Bloomington, IN 47403 USA
www.authorhouse.co.uk
Phone: 0800.197.4150

Published by AuthorHouse 09/26/2016

ISBN: 978-1-5246-6389-6 (sc)
ISBN: 978-1-5246-6387-2 (hc)
ISBN: 978-1-5246-6388-9 (e)

Print information available on the last page.

Any people depicted in stock imagery provided by Thinkstock are models, and such images are being used for illustrative purposes only.
Certain stock imagery © Thinkstock.

This book is printed on acid-free paper.

Because of the dynamic nature of the Internet, any web addresses or links contained in this book may have changed since publication and may no longer be valid. The views expressed in this work are solely those of the author and do not necessarily reflect the views of the publisher, and the publisher hereby disclaims any responsibility for them.

DEDICATION

I dedicate this book to every single person who wants to succeed; we are all students of a teacher called life, and this book is dedicated to those who want to learn from the life lessons given to us.

This is for every person who has ever had a dream.

For every young person who has ever looked at the TV and said, "I hope that can be me one day", for every young person who has sang along to R-Kelly's *The World's Greatest* and meant every single word.

I dedicate this book to every single person who wants to have a prosperous future – I dedicate this book to you to help you get there.

ACKNOWLEDGEMENTS

This book is all about life lessons – and therefore it is only right that I acknowledge the people who have impacted my growth and who have helped me learn so much in my 19 years of living. After all, if you surround yourself with great people, great things will happen to you! I am grateful for many of the people in my life, but I am also thankful for every single person who has come into my life to help me grow and to teach me something new.

Before I mention anyone else, I must first give all glory to God. Through his grace I am here, through his grace this book has been published, and through his grace you are reading this right now. I thank God for giving me the wisdom, knowledge, and confidence to put this book together and for fulfilling his promise – *Jeremiah 29:11*. God has given me a future full of hope and prosperity, so thank you God.

- My mentors, you have taught me everything I needed to know. You have been with me throughout this whole journey and you have kept me sane. Thank you to Nathaniel Peat for dedicating your time, for teaching me certain things about myself, and for showing me how to excel in life. Thank you to Junior Ogunyemi, who gave me the vision not only to write a book but to publish it in under six weeks. You also gave me the vision to start my own business, giving me the belief that I could do whatever I wanted regardless of age

– it is nothing but a number. Thank you also to Edwina Momoh. You have always kept me focused and disciplined, and you believed in me so much that in turn I was able to believe in myself. You have taught me how to break out of the box and reach for my dreams! May God bless you all.

- My extended family, Jackson Ogunyemi and Alim Kamara. You two have been my best friends, my adopted family, my angels and my champion companions. I am who I am today because of you two, so thank you for dedicating your life, time, love, and efforts to me. You have heard me cry, seen me smile, and heard me scream. You two have held my hand every step of the way – promising not to leave my side – and not once have you forsaken me. Jackson, when I was nine you became one of my superheroes, and Alim, when I was 15 you made me realise my calling. Both of you together have allowed me to become the woman, speaker, and business owner I am today, and may God bless you two abundantly.

- My squad Fiona, Javen, Ryan, Darnell and Olivia – you have all been with me through thick and thin, supporting me through the highs and the lows. Great friends are not those who want to be with you in the limousine, but they are the ones who will walk with you when the limousine breaks down – thank you for walking with me, throughout all of the trials and throughout all of the success. Fiona, you have been my backbone through it all, and I want to really say thank you for everything you have done for me; you are truly my sister for life. I love you Fiona. Javen you have also been my rock through it all, thank you for standing by me brother. May God bless you all.

- Thank you to Tobi Arayomi and Nicola Arayomi for planting the seed of Christ within me – you have both taught me the true meaning of fellowship and contributed to my spiritual growth in such a tremendous but humbling way. Thank you for believing in me and

making me realise my self worth. You have now become family and role models that I dearly love, respect and look up to. May God bless you both abundantly.
- My late father Mule, the stories I have heard about you are beautiful, and whilst growing up, everyone constantly told me I looked just like you. I have always said that when we meet again, you will say you're proud of me, so I am hoping that you are proud of me, Daddy. May you rest in peace.
- My older cousin Olivia, for teaching me everything I needed to know whilst growing up, and for raising me whilst Mummy was at work and Marvyn was at school – not only are you my big sister, but an incredibly important figure in my life. You have taught me priceless lessons, have shown me how to be strong, and have blessed me with Lebron and Jarell, who continuously bring joy to my life. God bless you and the kids.
- My God-sister Brenda, for being an important role model in my life, and for keeping me on track whilst growing up. If I didn't have someone like you to look up to, I know I wouldn't be who I am today. May God bless you.
- My little brother Joel, you have much to learn and I hope that I will be able to aid you and guide you as you make your way through life. As you grow, my love grows for you too. I am proud of the man you are becoming, even though you are my little brother. May God bless you.
- My older sister Josfin, even though you are thousands of miles away, you have always been quick to teach me about different things in life. Distance will never stop me loving you or from learning from you. May God bless you.
- My older brother Marvyn. Having my dad pass away at three years old led to you stepping in as the father figure in my life, and you have taught me well. You, Olivia, and Mummy taught me everything I needed to know growing up, so thank you for believing in me, for

being my best friend and the best big brother, and also for standing in as a dad. May God bless you.

- Finally, to my Mother, my Mummy and my rock. Being a single parent isn't easy but everything I do is for you. Every life lesson is first learnt at home and you have taught me the best life lessons yet – you have not only taught me how to grow through life, but you were also the person who taught me my alphabet, so if this book is to be summarised in just one person, it's you. May God bless you; may he give you long life, prosperity, and abundance, Mummy – I love you.

PREFACE

Let me not lie to you and say as we grow through life, that life will get easier. As you grow, so will the battles, but DON'T BE SCARED – as the battles grow, so do the blessings and as the blessings grow, so do the lessons.

One thing I have learned is that life can only get on top of you if you allow it to, and as a student, this is just the beginning of your journey to success. This journey is going to be a rollercoaster; sometimes you'll be screaming because of excitement, while at other times you'll be anxious because you don't know what's happening next, and more than likely you would rather just get off the ride to avoid anything bad from happening to you. As a student myself – both a university student and a student of life – I know that in this life, you live and you learn.

I have already learnt a lot, and I realised how easy it can be to forget important daily life lessons – especially the ones that will enhance us and help us get to the next level. They always say that the best way to overcome something is to go back to the basics, and what is more basic than the alphabet? The first thing you ever learn as a student is the alphabet, and it is something you will simply never forget, whether you're three years old or 35! The alphabet will be stuck in your head for life, but why? Why is it that we can be so quick to forget the daily life lessons that we actually use in life, but we will never forget the alphabet? This book is here to interlink the concept of the alphabet with life lessons.

With this book, students will be able to gain a deeper understanding and different perspective of the alphabet, learning that there are even life lessons to be found in a simple nursery rhyme we were taught as children. The whole concept of the 'ABCs to Student Success' is to teach life-changing lessons, content and motivation, by using something everyone knows and remembers: the alphabet. If you link the unknown with the known, how can you truly forget?

INTRODUCTION

This book is a simple, smart, motivating, innovative, and competent guide that will ensure you are being pushed closer and closer to success through the concept of the alphabet. I wouldn't say this book is going to be your average personal development book, as it's coming with a little twist, but I can definitely guarantee that you will develop from it. Innovation means delivering something that already exists but in a different way. With this in mind, many stories, quotes, and concepts in this book exist in other books, but I will be delivering them in a new, unique way to help you understand them and implement them in your daily life. In this book, I also highlight other student experiences, not just mine alone. We as students all go through different circumstances but even though we experience different circumstances and we all have our own individual journey; the ABCs can still be applied to all of us.

I want you to **read a letter a day.** By committing yourself to one letter each day, you will have just one topic to reflect on, to meditate on and expand on – it's important that you focus on just one thing at a time, as focusing on too many things can confuse you and can even cause a delay in your development. Take your time: there is NO RUSH, and growth happens at your own pace. Success is not a destination but a journey, so let's take this journey step by step and day by day, TOGETHER.

"Don't rush the process, what appears to be 'slow' or 'long' is actually necessary for your destination" – **Doctor Kanayo.**

So, you're about to start, and I need to mention here that I do have a few rules. Now, you see this book? I want you to keep it very close to your heart, because I'm telling you right now that everything is about to change.

RULE NUMBER 1.

Get yourself a pen and notepad because I don't want you to just read the following pages and then simply move on with your life. NO. Day by day and step by step we will plan, evaluate, and elevate YOU to the next level! So make sure you have your pens and pad ready to go.

RULE NUMBER 2.

HIGHLIGHT, LIVE, AND DEVOUR THIS BOOK. This is your one-way ticket to student success, and not only will you learn some valuable life lessons, but you will also learn more about yourself. This WILL enhance you and take you to the next level.

RULE NUMBER 3.

As you go through this book, share your journey with me!
I want to know how it's going, I want to know how you're feeling, and I want to read your testimonies. What has this book made you realise? Or how has a certain letter made you feel?
You can share it publically if you want via social media using the hashtag **#ABC2SS**

Mention me on **Twitter @HaylsMulenda**
Instagram - @HaylsMule

WHY I WROTE THIS BOOK

In sixth form I studied psychology, and the way in which my psychology teacher taught me the subject was incredibly interesting; he related it back to life, making me realise how psychology really does play an important role and impact upon everyday life. There was one strategy he taught me in terms of memory improvement: The Method of Loci, which consists of interlinking items that you're trying to remember with your own household. So, for instance, you can place these items across your living room, and whenever you imagine your living room, you will remember the items because you put them in a memorable place. The whole concept of this book is an innovative version of the Method of Loci; the life lessons are jotted around the alphabet because the alphabet is something we can all remember, and the life lessons are what we *need* to remember.

It was January 1st 2016 and I had just left church. In the car on the way back I told myself that 2016 was going to be a prosperous year, and I promised myself I was going to make a change. In February, however, after winning the biggest award of my life, getting loads of bookings for my motivational speaking, and taking part in several different interviews, it all started to get rather overwhelming – I just couldn't cope. I had pressure from my business, my family, university, my friends, and from society in general. Everything was going wrong for me and I just didn't know what to do; for once, the motivational speaker needed motivation. I had to put up this front that I was okay even though I wasn't, and this unfortunately led me to becoming suicidal and having a mental breakdown. I missed university for roughly two whole months, and within those two months I had my mentors, family, and friends helping me out of my dark place. I learned different lessons from every single one of them, helping me cope not only with university but with life in general. I guess everyone puts up this front to keep people out – it's life.

Fortunately, I got to a better place, and within a few months Hayley was Hayley again. Those life lessons I learned were so powerful that I realised I wanted to share them with the world, whether to help young people who were going through major problems, or to help those who were just going through minor problems – I knew these life lessons would have a positive effect either way!

One month before my 19th birthday, I was on the phone to one of my mentors, Nathaniel Peat, when he asked me, "Where is your book?" and "Why are you taking so long?" He gave me a deadline and I realised I had just six weeks to write it. And, while it wasn't easy, I was DETERMINED to finish it. Why? Because me being in a bad place and learning all of those life lessons had made me realise that I probably wasn't the only person who forgets these types of life lessons when we actually need them, and that sometimes we need others to help us through it. I want to help as many people as I can, so I prayed on it, praying very hard and wondering how I could create a book that would relate to students/young people, that could help them in life, and that could help them implement a concept they will never forget. I prayed on it for a long time, and God delivered. He gave me the title, the idea, and the concept for this book.

So, I was determined to have this whole book written up, designed, edited, proofread, published, and printed. The journey hasn't been easy, but no journey worth taking ever *is* easy, and sometimes that journey can be lonely – personally, I had to sacrifice certain events and distance myself from certain people, even loved ones, but this meant I could focus on finishing the book. One thing I've realised in this life is that there is a price to pay, and you have to be willing to pay that price in order to get the prize. This price is always expensive, and it will HURT; you will have to invest money that will hurt your bank account, be distant from people you love, and even cut off certain programmes you love, but it's all worth it in the end! Another thing I've realised is that if you want to stand out from the crowd, you can't simply follow the crowd, and by reading this book, you will learn exactly *how* you can stand out from the crowd.

Now, I think it's time we actually move on to the book! Let me just say that I am so proud of you for taking time out of your day to improve yourself and to evolve to the next level! I am with you every step of the way, and so is God – may he guide you as you start this beautiful journey. I am so excited for you! **SO LET'S GO!**

A – ACCEPTANCE

Acceptance – Embracing what is rather than wishing for something that is not.

"What you deny or ignore, you delay. What you accept and face, you conquer"

– Robert Tew.

A is the first letter of the alphabet; this right here is now the starting point for you and the first step of your journey; you are one step closer to where you want to be, one step closer to where you *need* to be.

Now, in order for you to evolve to the next level, you must first accept your current level – before you can reach the finishing line, you need to have a starting point. Ask yourself the following questions: where do I want to go? What do I want to accomplish? **Where am I now?**

Before Steve Harvey became a successful Comedian, TV host, Author, and Motivational Speaker, he was in a dead-end job that he hated, but he knew that first he had to accept his current situation in order to elevate himself to his next destination. If he hadn't accepted the fact he was unhappy in that job, he would've never quit and made that essential change in his life.

We, as students, all go through certain trials in our everyday lives, such as difficult assignments, procrastination, or even a difficult teacher/lecturer, and sometimes we are too scared to accept those trials, which is EXACTLY how procrastination starts.

"Procrastination is the thief of time" **– Edward Young.**

Sometimes we don't want to accept the task that's there, which leads us to delay it until the last minute, causing us to rush it whilst downing cup after cup of coffee and screaming, **'GOD, WHY ME?'**

Quick Q: How do we expect to find a solution when we have not acknowledged or accepted the problem?

We are so quick to talk about where we want to go, but why are we *not* so quick to talk about where we currently are? It reminds me of when you're about to meet up with a friend and they call up, asking, "Where are you?" and you reply that you're around the corner even though you haven't actually left your house yet. Well, this idea can also be applied to your goals: if success was to call you up and ask, "Where are you?", how would you reply? Are you just around the corner? Or are you still in your house?

"Every building in the world starts from the ground floor" – **Hayley Mulenda.**

A prime example of the harsh realities of acceptance comes about on results day. Why is this day so scary? Because it's the day where you HAVE to accept what's on that paper, with no ifs and no buts – the examiners always have the final say.

A level results day was an incredibly daunting day; you saw people crying who you'd never seen cry in your entire life, and the people who always had something to say were as quiet as a mouse. But that day was also a powerful day – and not just for me but for others too – because that was the day when we had to accept where we'd gone wrong, when we had to acknowledge our mistakes and then use those lessons to enhance us, not destroy us.

REFLECTION TIME

Get your journal ready! Now it's time to write and reflect.

Answer these questions for me, and remember to be honest with yourself – the worst thing you could ever do is lie to yourself.

What is your final destination/end goal? (P.S. make sure you dream big – how can the sky be the limit when there are footprints on the moon?)

What is your current situation/starting point?

How are you hoping to change your current situation to ensure you reach your final destination?

TASK

Take a piece of paper and draw a line down the middle (leaving enough space at the top and the bottom of the paper for you to write). At the very top of the paper describe where you want to be, and at the bottom describe where you are now. Now, look at the gap – you have a fair way to go, and before you can start the journey, you need to accept that it's going to be a long one. However, although it won't be easy, it won't be impossible either.

What did you learn from this chapter? How has it helped you? Why don't you tell us on social media!

DON'T FORGET TO USE THE HASHTAG #ABC2SS - @HaylsMulenda

B – BLESSINGS

Blessings – The things that you have in your life that you're not meant to have, but you have them anyway because you've been blessed with them.

"God gave you a gift of 84,600 seconds today. Have you used one of them to say thank you?" — **William Arthur Ward.**

You cannot move onto the next chapter until you have summarised the last one, and I'm not just talking about the book here, but about life as well. So, before we move onto each chapter, this book will always summarise the last one.

Acceptance allows you to move on and to acknowledge the blessings you have in your life, so ask yourself this: have you been able to accept everything that's going on in your life?

Now, let's talk about your blessings. The best attitude to have in life is the attitude of gratitude. How do you expect God to give you more blessings when you're not even saying thank you for the blessings you already have?

It's like when you're giving a baby milk from the bottle; if they spit out the milk and refuse to open their mouth, you immediately start to think, 'well, this baby isn't hungry. I'm not going to force the milk down its throat!' and that's how it is with God. Sometimes God gives us blessings, and if you're spitting them out, you're not saying 'thank you', and therefore

God may refrain from blessing you even more – after all, why would God give you more blessings if you're spitting out the ones you already have?

You are highly blessed and it's imperative that you realise this. The fact you have LIFE alone is such a powerful blessing, and the fact that God woke you up today highlights that you still have a purpose – YOU are still a blessing yourself. Are you going to waste your purpose simply because you want to focus on your problems rather than your blessings?

Whatever you focus on, will also focus on you. Have you ever noticed that when you focus on your problems, they get bigger? Bigger than they actually are? Now, imagine if you could do that with your blessings instead. Focus on your blessings and they will get bigger. Focus on your problems and they will follow you – but if you focus on your blessings, they will follow you too. We all have problems and we all have blessings, but one thing I do want you to understand is that it's YOUR choice as to which thing you will focus on; it's up to you whether you want to focus on your blessings or whether you want to focus on your problems. I personally chose to focus on my blessings, and now I realise that I'm too blessed to be stressed – the fact that I can see, walk, talk, breathe, have a house, have clothes on my back... the list goes on. Even though we all have our problems, remember this: they could be 10 times WORSE! So, always try to look on the brighter side of life – you lose nothing counting your blessings, but you can lose so much when counting your problems.

We take so much for granted and therefore it's really important that we start to appreciate what we have in our life – appreciation is key. Gratitude is one of the best qualities you can have, and people will respect you more if you have the quality of gratitude in your life. This life is unpredictable, and I always say, "Focus on the blessings you *have* before they turn into the blessings you *had*."

REFLECTION TIME

Think about your blessings.

What modules/subjects are you gifted in?

TASK

Start every morning with a thank you; you're highly blessed and the least you can do is say 'thank you' to God.

What did you learn from this chapter? How has it helped you? Why don't you tell us on social media!

DON'T FORGET TO USE THE HASHTAG #ABC2SS - @HaylsMulenda

C – CONFIDENCE

Confidence – A feeling of trust, faith, and belief in yourself or others.

"The most beautiful thing you can wear is confidence" – **Blake Lively.**

Blessings can help you become confident simply because some of the blessings you have in your life are unique, which make you special and one of a kind. So, own it and be confident about it!

Confidence means knowing you are special and feeding off it so that you're able to grow through life. One thing that many people have told me I have a lot of is confidence, and this is one thing that many people lack in life, so let me help you enhance YOUR confidence! Sometimes people get mixed up between confidence and cockiness, and there is a thin line between the two – just make sure you don't cross that line!

Confidence is internal; through confidence, you are feeding off your own faiths and beliefs in order to know your worth and to know that you are amazing. Confidence is associated with humility – you are not trying to pull others down, ONLY to pull yourself up. "But how do I pull myself up?" you may ask. Well it's by understanding that you are wonderfully and fearfully made. God CREATED you in his image, not the image of the animals, the sea, or the angels, but in HIS image. You are a powerful, amazing, and great being because you come from a powerful, amazing, and great God. I am very confident within myself, simply because when I wake up in the morning and look in the mirror, I am the person I have to see. After all, I live with myself 24/7, so I need to feel good about myself and big myself up, because no one else will. Have you ever noticed how the best music performers are the performers who feed off their own energy? The crowd could be completely dead, but because they're confident within themselves, they STILL give an amazing performance – that's how it is in real life. Sometimes you're going to have to feed off your own confidence rather than looking to others, because not everyone is going to support you.

Cockiness, on the other hand, is relying on others to know your worth, and it is associated with arrogance, and with having to reveal/exaggerate your abilities and importance in order to understand your self worth. With cockiness you are trying to pull others down to pull yourself up, and you should never pull others down; no one is better than anyone else in this world – we all have the same 24 hours a day, meaning we are all the same. Yes, others may have more money, but nothing is more powerful than time.

You may be given an assignment, and in order to do it you are going to have to be confident within yourself, because if you don't take that task on confidently, you will end up giving up, and giving up **shouldn't** an option! There is an 'I' in confidence for a reason, and if *you* don't claim it, no one else will. Go through life with your head held high – no one wants to talk to someone who has their head to their ground, but everyone wants to talk to the person who has their head pointed to the sky. Through confidence you will allow a light to form within you, and when a light is formed from within, you attract others around you – everyone notices light within a dark room, and as this world is so dark, aim to be the light rather than being consumed by the darkness.

I will tell you one thing, my mum was TOTALLY against me starting my own business and becoming a motivational speaker – she wanted me to become a teacher with a more stable job – but I knew that my purpose wasn't for me to be a teacher within a school, but a teacher amongst a nation. I had to put up with backlash from my mum, left right and centre, until she started to see how much I believed in myself. And it wasn't just my mum but my mentors and my friends around me as well; I had many people telling me that I wouldn't be able to become a speaker. People just wouldn't listen to me, and while I could have fed off their negative energy and started to believe what they were telling me, I didn't – I fed off my own energy, believing in *myself*, and it worked. The same people who doubted me (including my mum!) are now the same people who support me. Through confidence I was able to make myself stand out, getting booking after booking, and award after award. And all because I believed in myself, which led to other people actually believing in me too!

What's within you is far more powerful than anything that is around you. IT ALL STARTS WITH YOU.

Confidence isn't walking into a room and thinking you're better than anyone else; confidence is walking into a room and knowing that there is no one like you. Feed off your own confidence – it'll never run out.

REFLECTION TIME

What are you lacking confidence in and why?
What are you confident about in your life right now?

TASK

Stand in front of a mirror and give yourself a pep talk! Tell yourself how important you are and how you can do this – and *make sure you mean it.* The best person to motivate you is yourself!

What did you learn from this chapter? How has it helped you? Why don't you tell us on social media!

DON'T FORGET TO USE THE HASHTAG #ABC2SS - @HaylsMulenda

D – DETERMINATION

Determination – Doing what needs to be done even when you don't want to do it.

"You can and you WILL. END OF STORY" – **Unknown.**

Determination is having CONFIDENCE within the journey, and confidence that you will finish what you started; in life you HAVE to be determined, and you have to feel confident enough to make sure you finish what you've started.

Determination is the fuel – it's what will help you get to where you need to be. It will get you from plan A to B to C, and then on to the end of the alphabet and this book.

When it comes to determination I want to highlight one of my best friend's experiences as to how determination got him to where he is now, Darnell has now worked with different big UK artists across the scene but where he is now is not just down to acceptance, blessings, and confidence but his determination. His current destination is due to his previous determination. Darnell started filming in sixth-form and was determined to get himself out there, to get recognised and to build within his craft. Videography/ editing equipment are not cheap, his passion led to him working part time and sometimes full time in a job that he hated. Darnell had to balance a job he hates and sixth-form just so he could invest in professional equipment which will help build his. Now remember we have defined determination as 'doing what needs to be done even when you don't want to do it' Darnell had to commit time to a job he hated so he could make money to invest in something he was passionate about. After working all those hours in his dead-end job, he was able to save enough money to buy professional equipment but he also had to sacrifice certain motives because he knew that balancing work, sixth form and motives will be impossible – that's not something he wanted to do but it was needed. Darnell has now worked with MCs such as Chip, Ghetts, and others on Revolt TV. This wouldn't have been possible if he wasn't determined to commit himself to the things he needed to do to get the things he wanted to have.

Sometimes you are going to have to do things you don't want to do but you need to do. As I stated before there is always a price to pay, if you want the prize – be determined to pay that price.

Now for all you film fanatics let me relate determination to two of my favourite films; *Finding Nemo* and *Finding Dory*. Now, this will be really awkward if you haven't watched them – so I hope you have – and if you haven't, GO WATCH AT LEAST ONE OF THEM ASAP!

Basically, Dory is a pacific blue tang fish with short-term memory loss. However, whenever Dory is thrown an obstacle, she is determined to overcome it, regardless of the fact that she can only remember something for 30 seconds. The one thing I have learned from Dory is 'Just Keep Swimming' – Dory kept swimming, even when she didn't know what she would face. She *did* know she would have to face trials and tribulations, but that didn't stop her; in fact, she was able to influence Marlon to have that exact same mentality, which led to him finding Nemo and to Dory finding her parents (sorry, I spoiled it, didn't I?)

In life you have to keep on swimming – you have to keep going regardless of what you are going through. Life is like a bicycle: to keep it balanced you must keep it moving.

Everything will be okay in the end, and if its not okay then it's NOT THE END. Be determined to see the end, because at the end of every rainbow there is a pot of gold. Now, do you REALLY want your pot of gold? Well, go and get it then!

"Determination determines your destination" – **Qwanda Frasier.**

The more you experience in life, the more experienced you will become, which in turn will fuel your determination. A boxer can't win a boxing match without having experienced an actual fight. Floyd Mayweather has won every fight he's ever participated in, and this is because he was determined to win every time he was in that ring.

You are now in that ring, and my question is: Are you determined to win?

REFLECTION TIME

What obstacles are you facing right now?

How determined are you to overcome them?

TASK

Write yourself a mini letter of encouragement, outlining what you are going through and stating that you *will* overcome it and conquer it! Get as personal as you want, and make sure you put your ALL into it because you are writing to yourself!

What did you learn from this chapter? How has it helped you?

Why don't you tell us on social media!

DON'T FORGET TO USE THE HASHTAG #ABC2SS - @HaylsMulenda

E – ENVIRONMENT

Environment – the space you surround yourself in, the space where you spend the most of your time.

"If it's not helping you grow, it's got to go"– **Hayley Mulenda.**

Determination is what you need to take you the whole way, but if you're in a bad environment in the first place, you may find it very hard to become truly determined – do you feel you're in a place that contributes to your determination or your distractions?

Do you expect a rose to grow in a garden full of weeds and bleach? No. You will never blossom in a toxic environment, so if you want to blossom, put yourself in an environment that is already blossoming.

The best way to learn a language is to surround yourself with people who are already speaking that language, so if you want to learn the language of success, surround yourself with people who already speak it.

Tai Lopez talks about the *rule of 33%* – he states that you spend 1% of your time daydreaming, and that you should spend 33% with people above you (e.g. mentors).

Mentors are people who are already experienced in what you want to do or where you want to go in life. They can save you a lot of time, as you can learn from the mistakes they've made, preventing you from making them in the first place. A lot of my growth has been because of my mentors dedicating their time, effort, and lessons to me, and allowing me to play my cards right. In a way, life is a game: you need to make the right moves, talk to the right people, and make the right decisions to go in the right direction – when you have mentors, ALL of that is possible.

My mentor Action Jackson's book (SHUT UP AND TAKE ACTION by Jackson Ogunyemi) –includes a chapter about mentorship and how to find the right mentor for you. Here are the tips he talked about:

1. *Read books and magazines in your chosen field and identify possible mentors, or you could even use social media!*

2. *List their names, skill level, and the impact they have made.*
3. *List what you want from that mentor.*
4. *Contact that mentor and arrange a meeting.*

Things to keep in mind before meeting a mentor:

1. Listen more than you talk – in a 2:1 ratio.

2. Always have a notebook to hand (take notes from what they're saying).
3. Always be on time for meetings (in fact, try and be early).
4. Emulate what they do: "Be a copycat. At least this cat is going somewhere."

The other 33% of your time should be spent with people below you. We rise by lifting others, so this could be someone who may need your help or someone whom you can, in fact, mentor – after all, the best way to live is to give. So be sure to give to others. I have four different mentees and each time we meet up or catch up, we break down how we can expand their growth. This isn't just a one-way street, however even though I'm helping them, they help me too. Some of my mentees are younger than me and some of them are older than me, but we all have a mutual respect for each other. You can learn from ANYONE regardless of their age, background, gender, or experiences; just because you're helping someone below you, it doesn't mean you have to remind them constantly that you're higher than them – humility will take you far.

The last 33% should be spent with people who are on your level, so your friends.

One of the biggest things I've learned is how much your friends impact your life; they have more influence on you than you may think.

"Tell me who your top 3 friends are and I will tell you whether you are going to be successful or not" – **Jackson Ogunyemi.**

Friend Cleanse – Is your friend REALLY your friend? I am always hearing, "friend this, friend that," but is your friend helping you grow? Elevate? Change for the better?

Your friend should tell you what you NEED to hear, not what you WANT to hear, and if they don't challenge you, they won't change you. Whatever you follow determines what follows you, so if you follow stupid people, stupid situations will follow you. Your friends are your neighbours, so if your postman is knocking on your friend's door and delivering L's, then guess whose door is getting knocked on next? You. If your friend is receiving blessings, guess who's receiving them next door? So be careful who you allow to be your neighbours. You are a product of your own environment.

"Whatever you follow determines what follows you" – **Action Jackson.**

I follow great people, meaning greatness follows me.

Action Jackson states that it's important you have a **CHAMPION COMPANION** – He has Alim Kamara. They both tour the world inspiring people to greatness, and they constantly challenge each other, help each other, motivate each other, and inspire each other.

A champion companion is a companion who is going to help you become a champion.

This person has to **challenge you, help you, inspire you, and motivate you** to keep going. You need someone who is going to be honest, who will show tough love, and who will discipline you. If you're able, find someone who will keep you in check, no matter what life throws at you.

My best friend Ryan constantly motivates me, inspires me, and keeps me going. His work ethic is amazing; he can easily revise for 20 hours straight if he wanted to. People become intimidated whilst revising with Ryan because they realise how much they need to fix up whilst sitting next to him – I have never met anyone who works as hard as Ryan does – and it inspires me to work harder too. Ryan's success motivates me, and in turn, my success motivates him. He has been recognised as one of the most outstanding top black students in the UK and I've been recognised as one of the Most Inspirational and Influential Black Entrepreneurs in the UK. He inspires me to do better and I inspire him to do better too! If I am feeling low he will give me a pep talk, if he is feeling low I do the same. Your champion companion has to be with you during the fall and glory. Be sure to surround yourself with others who will lift you up when you have fallen down. The one amazing thing is that Ryan isn't the only champion companion I have; ALL of my friends are my champion companions, they're all doing amazing things, and they all inspire me in different ways. I love being able to win with my people around me, it's beautiful to share success with the ones you love.

You enjoy a meal most when you're eating it with loved ones, don't you? There's enough space for all of us to be at the winning table, but just make sure that you're surrounding yourself with those who will help you *get* to that winning table in the first place.

Spend time with people who you can build with, not chill with.

I've had my fair share of bad company over the years, and it's crazy how when I started to drop certain people, certain blessings started to drop on me. Bad company can corrupt a good character and block blessings from you, the same way you need to delete irrelevant apps to free up space on your phone to store new apps is the same way you also need to delete irrelevant friends to free up your new blessings.

There are two type of friends – assets and liabilities. Assets mean you gain, whereas liabilities drain. Do you gain from your friends? Or do you find yourself drained by their company? Negative friends will drain you. Jealous friends will drain you. Friends that always want to gossip about others will drain you. Friends who only care about themselves will drain you. Don't surround yourself with those who will drain you. **LOVE YOURSELF** enough to surround yourself with people who will help you grow.

Earlier this year I had someone very close to me look me in the eye and tell me they didn't want me to be successful, due to jealousy this person done everything they could to try and ruin me mentally, emotionally and even physically. I loved this person dearly but I realised a few months ago sometimes even people you love have to go before you can grow. Be careful what type of environment you're in, it has a huge impact on your success. Negative people lead you to negative situations.

Another reason as to why your environment is important is because your environment may also limit your opportunities, and for this I want to talk about koi fish, which is a Japanese fish and a great example as to how your environment can have a big effect on you.

If you put a koi fish in a small fish tank, it will grow to only four inches. This is because it adapts to its environment, and a small tank will only allow it to grow to four inches. If, however, you take that koi fish and place it into a bigger fish tank, the koi fish will grow to 8 inches. If you take it out of the bigger fish tank and put it in the pond, it will grow to 18 inches, and if you take it out of the pond and put it in a lake, it will grow to 42 inches.

So, a koi fish has the potential to be 42 inches long, but it only grows that big if it's in an environment that *allows* it to grow that big.

Are you in an environment that's allowing you to grow that big?

REFLECTION TIME

Name your friends that are draining.

Name your friends that you benefit from.

How will you improve your environment?

TASK

Get some paper and draw a line down the middle. On one side write 'gain' and on the other side write 'drain'. Now, write down all of the things that drain you in your environment and then write down all of the things that you gain from being in your environment.

What did you learn from this chapter? How has it helped you?

Why don't you tell us on social media!

DON'T FORGET TO USE THE HASHTAG #ABC2SS - @HayIsMulenda

F – FULL TIME

Full Time – Occupying or using the whole of someone's available working time.

"If you put in a full time grind, you will get full time results" – **Hayley Mulenda.**

You have to be dedicated in life to get to where you want to be, however, it's not just about being determined but about being committed too! You have to put in maximum work to get maximum results.

Do you expect full time pay when you work part time hours? No! So why expect full time results with a part time grind?

What you put in is exactly what you get out. Many times we want something but we just won't put in the work to get it – NOTHING comes easy in life. If you want six-pack abs, you need to go and WORK OUT. If you want a good grade, you need to PUT in good hours! I have quite a toned stomach now, but it didn't come easy – I had to have a strict diet and do intense training so that I could tone it up! Nothing good comes easy in life, and if it *has* come easy, it's probably not good.

I have been on my motivational speaking journey for three years now. In September 2013, Action Jackson came into my school to conduct a motivational talk, and it was on that day that I decided I wanted to motivate people for the rest of my life. These past three years haven't been easy – I've had people turn me down, people leave me, and people betray me – but those obstacles couldn't stop me from carrying on! I had to keep going simply because friction means you are moving. However, the only way for you to move is if you dedicate yourself full time to making that movement work and to go forward.

You reap what you sow – real talk.

I know some of you may be reading this and thinking, 'I *do* put in the work, but I don't see the results.' Now, being full time doesn't just mean that you're working hard, but that you're also working smart.

"What's working smart, Hayley?" Don't worry, I'll break it down for you.

Sometimes in life, we work hard on something that will take us nowhere and that will not elevate us at all. It's about being productive and not just proactive. If you're being proactive, you can read and finish a book you need to read, but if you're productive, you will be highlighting, taking notes, and playing memory games so that you're able to remember what you've read.

"If you want to be successful in the long run, you have to be willing to do a long run" – **Hayley Mulenda.**

I love chess, and the reason why I love it is because the concept of that game can be applied to life. In chess, you always have to be 10 steps ahead of your opponent – if you're not 10 steps ahead, you will lose. You do not GO through life; you GROW through life. You grow through your thoughts and not your actions.

"Yeah, but Hayley, our actions create the steps to success, don't they?" Yes, but what triggers your actions? Your thoughts.

A full time grind allows you to not get complacent, as complacency is incredibly dangerous. If you get complacent, SOMEONE will take your placement. To commit yourself to a full time grind, you will see full time sweat, blood, and tears, but you will also reap the full time blessings, good news, and congratulations.

REFLECTION TIME

Are you putting in enough time towards your goals?

How committed are you? How much commitment do you actually need?

TASK

Watch **Nego True – Hunger** (YOUTUBE)

What did you learn from this chapter? How has it helped you?

Why don't you tell us on social media!

DON'T FORGET TO USE THE HASHTAG #ABC2SS - @HaylsMulenda

G – GET GOD

Get God – to connect with the ultimate source – the father and creator – because in order to get great things, you need to engage with the Great God.

"For I know the plans I have for you declares the Lord, plans to prosper you not harm you, plans to give you a hope and future" – **Jeremiah 29:11.**

Why expect full time blessings when you're going just part time with God? If you're full time in God, I know he will be full time in you. He's the best thing to be full time in!

One thing I have learned this year is that before you can find success, you need to find the person who actually allows it to happen: God. It is true that many of us are spiritually dead. You would never leave your house with a dead phone, so why would you leave your house with a dead spirit? You will delay your friends to charge your phone for an extra 10 minutes, so why wouldn't you do that to charge your spirit for 10 minutes with prayer?

I am a firm believer in God, not just because I've had my own personal experience with him but because I've seen him work with many others around me too. I can definitely testify and say that God has interceded in many tests I've faced in my life, and also that he converted my tests to testimony. So, let me break down the importance of getting God.

When an iPhone breaks down, you don't take it to Samsung to fix it – you take it to Apple. Why? Because Apple manufactured that product and Apple knows the product in far more detail than Samsung does. No one knows the product better than the manufacturer, whether that be how to fix it if something goes wrong, or how to improve it in general. God is OUR manufacturer, so he knows how to fix us and how to improve us. God is the creator, so he creates success and he creates opportunity. Why plug into the world that feeds off success? Plug into the creator who actually provides it. God is the source, and everything else that's good in this life is a resource – if you want the resources, you must first connect with the source.

Jeremiah 29:11 is my favourite Bible verse, as this shows us that when the WORLD breaks us, God wants to build us again. There is not one thing that God hasn't pulled us through, and if he hasn't pulled you through yet, he is PULLING you through right now. Honestly, God has done so much for me this year, it would be rude to tell you to Get God and not talk about why I have committed myself to him.

Early this year, I had a massive breakdown. I couldn't cope with university, I had close ones betray me, and people who I never thought would leave me did just that. I started to work TOO hard, balancing a course I hated with motivational speaking, which is what I loved. However, because I spent more time in university than on the thing I loved doing, I would always ask myself, "WHY AM I HERE?" I started to feel really lonely at university, and I even experienced racism on campus – it was crazy.

After everything had piled up, I broke. I literally broke down, becoming depressed and anxious – I missed university for two months, and I was in and out of hospital. I didn't like talking to anyone – not even my own mother – and after a few days of being in a bad place, the suicidal thoughts started to come, regardless of the fact that one month before I had literally won the biggest award of my life. This just goes to show that while awards and materialistic things can fill the void, they can never make you happy.

My brother had to call me whilst he was at work from 9am – 5pm, and my best friend Fiona had to call me whilst she was studying in the library from 6pm – 12am. People were literally taking shifts to make sure I wouldn't kill myself. To cut a long story short, I finally had enough of being down, enough of being depressed, and enough of being anxious to the extent that I couldn't leave my house or EVEN my room. I was sick and tired of being sick and tired. One night I cried out to God asking him to help me, to save me, and honestly, I felt a warm, fuzzy feeling inside as something just lifted off me. I was literally on the edge, if I didn't pray that night I may have actually killed myself but that warm fuzzy feeling gave me hope. I can't really describe that feeling but it was a feeling that made me feel comforted, loved and admired. After that encounter, day-by-day, I could start to feel myself getting back to my usual self. It didn't happen in just one day – it happened over the period of three months – but it was a miracle indeed. God took me from my own suicidal thoughts to saving eight suicidal young people this summer. My experience of being in a bad place has allowed me to become a better speaker, a more powerful storyteller, and just a stronger individual in general. God will change you, if you allow him to.

In prayer you need to **PUSH:**

Pray
Until
Something
Happens.

Prayer isn't always there to change the situation, but to actually change *you*. If you want God to change the circumstances around you, allow him to first change you.

REFLECTION TIME

Are you currently happy with your relationship with God?

Ask yourself the following questions:

"What can I do to get closer to God?"

"Am I trying to please God or others?"

"Do I care more about the world or more about God?"

"Follow your calling, not the crowd!" – **Sarah Oladokun.**

Many times we allow this world to lead us astray. Don't follow the world, God is the way.

For those of you who don't know how to find God, or haven't got a relationship with God yet, read **Jeremiah 29:13.**

TASK

Put your phone down and get away from all social media. Put EVERYTHING away and have your own time with God, one on one. Why don't you put some time aside today to really connect with him?

What did you learn from this chapter? How has it helped you?

Why don't you tell us on social media!

DON'T FORGET TO USE THE HASHTAG #ABC2SS - @HaylsMulenda

H – HEALTH

Health – The state of being free from illness or injury, both physically and mentally.

"Your health is your wealth" – **Unknown.**

Getting right with God allows you to become healthier spiritually, and while spiritual health is very important, you also need to balance the other states you have – the physical and mental states.

You would probably be a millionaire by now if you got a pound for every time you heard the words, "your health is your wealth," right? Well, let me add another pound to that account.

Your success is limited in a hospital bed; trust me, I would know. I've been in and out of hospital before, having blood test after blood test and ECG after ECG, and it wasn't easy. I had to cancel all of my motivational talks, I couldn't go to university for two months, and it affected me mentally too (as you read in chapter G, where I mentioned my testimony).

It is really important that you take your health seriously, because when you're healthy you're able to focus on actually becoming successful, but if your health starts to get in the way, it can cause big distractions or delays. Of course, I do understand that some health conditions can't be helped because they're generational, however, prevention is better than cure – we can't cure that illness now, BUT we can prevent it from getting any worse.

Most people feel that health is about their physical state, and while that may be true, it's not *just* about keeping up with your physical health but with your mental health as well. Health starts on the inside, so feed your mind with seeds, not weeds – feed your mind with things that will help it grow.

MENTAL HEALTH IMPROVEMENT

Good music – listen to music that makes you feel good and makes you feel right! Good tunes allow good vibes!

Good company – we've already talked about how much your environment impacts your health, so make sure you are in a good environment with good company.

Good release – make sure you are releasing your emotions, whether that means having someone to talk to or having somewhere to write your issues down. It's not good to bottle ANYTHING IN!

If you want someone to talk to or would just like some guidance in general, here are some good contacts:

Tweet @HFNE_
www.hfne.co
http://www.samaritans.org/

PHYSICAL HEALTH IMPROVEMENT

Eat clean to reach your dreams!

I always ensure that the first thing I eat every day is fruit, granola, and chai seeds. Granola/chai seeds/Weetabix/oats are very good carbohydrates because they are slow releasing, meaning that they'll provide you with good energy throughout the day.

I remember in sixth form that I used to go into classes without having breakfast, and that actually led to me falling asleep in my lessons! So trust me when I say your breakfast has a BIG impact on your concentration levels throughout the day – ever since I started eating breakfast, I've become more energetic, happier, and far more bubbly!

If you start your day with the wrong food – or *no* food – you will have the wrong energy – or *no* energy – throughout the day. It's been scientifically proven that you're not able to function properly without having (a good) breakfast.

Get some rest!

Sleep is very important too, as having a good amount of sleep every night allows you to rest your body well. Throughout the day our body goes through so much, and it needs to rest in order to restore what it's lost during the day. Studies have shown that the most successful people have a set bedtime and a set amount of hours that they try and sleep for every night.

Exercise more!

This doesn't have to be hard: you can simply walk more instead of taking the bus or the train, and you can try to engage in more physical activities generally. An important note to make here is that if you're increasing your exercise, DRINK MORE WATER.

One summer I went out without water and I got so dizzy I dropped to the floor. My friend had to rush me to the shop to get me water, and I learned my lesson – I'm never doing that again.

REFLECTION TIME

What can you do to be more mentally healthy?
What can you do to be more physically healthy?

TASK

Write a fruit plan: plan which fruits you will eat every day for a week, and it'll soon get into your routine.

What did you learn from this chapter? How has it helped you? Why don't you tell us on social media!

DON'T FORGET TO USE THE HASHTAG #ABC2SS - @HaylsMulenda

I – INVESTMENT

Investment – To provide/endow with the aim to gain profit.

"The investments we make in ourselves will always deliver the most profitable returns." – **Sumner Davenport.**

Investing in your health is very important. As investment is about putting in something and gaining more out of it, so what better things to invest in than something that will allow you to live a better life? Investment is crucial in life, but is what you're investing in yourself actually benefitting you? What are you investing your money into? Is the money you're spending contributing to your personal development?

When we think of investment we usually think of money, but instead of buying materialistic things, why not look at self-investment and invest in your own growth? By buying materialistic things you are purchasing liabilities, and liabilities drain you and drain your account. With assets, YOU GAIN.

Let me just say how proud I am of you for purchasing this book, because through this book you are investing – investing in yourself, and investing in your greatness.

When you invest in external things (trainers, coats, bags, etc.) you may attach your self worth to those materialistic items, so once those items go, there's a possibility that some of your self worth will go with them. External things are limited; internal things are unlimited. Feed your soul, NOT your ego.

Two great examples of how investment truly works are Usain Bolt and doctors. Bolt has the treble treble, which means that for the past three Olympic Games, he has won gold three times. So, 3x3. In the latest three Olympics, he has run for less than two minutes, but from that success he has been able to make over 100 million dollars. We need to remember that even though he ran for just two minutes, he has trained for 25 years. By investing 25 years and only running for two minutes, Usain Bolt has become a multi-millionaire. NOW THAT'S WHAT YOU CALL INVESTMENT.

Doctors are able to diagnose and prescribe medication in under five minutes, but they have had to dedicate over 10 years of their life in order to do that. They invested 10 years in order to do everything in five minutes.

REFLECTION TIME

Invest in yourself internally: Invest in your intelligence – what books are you buying? What events are you attending to increase your knowledge?

Invest in your health: What healthy foods are you investing in? What physical activities are you putting your money towards?

Invest in your talents: What classes are you taking to improve your talents/career? What workshops are you attending in order to improve your gifts?

Invest in yourself spiritually: What money are you putting towards your spiritual growth and growing with God?

TASK

Write down how much money you're left with each month after fixed costs (rent, bills etc.) Now draw four boxes, and in those four boxes you will split your income:

40% of your monthly allowance should be savings.
20% of your monthly allowance should be investment.
30% of your monthly allowance should be pleasure (e.g. shopping).
10% of your monthly allowance should be tithe.

What did you learn from this chapter? How has it helped you? Why don't you tell us on social media!

DON'T FORGET TO USE THE HASHTAG #ABC2SS - @HaylsMulenda

J – JUMP

Jump – Taking the leap of faith.

"If I can see it, then I can do it, If I just believe it, there's nothing to it – I BELIEVE I CAN FLY" – **R. Kelly (R. Kelly – I Believe I Can Fly).**

The whole aim of investment is to make a profit, and another way for you to profit in this life is to take risks! You're going to HAVE to jump and take the leap of faith.

In order to get the things you don't have, you must do things you wouldn't normally do. You're going to have to take the risk, and the best way to see is to see with faith and not by sight. Faith allows you to trust in that 1% of success, rather than that 99% of failure – even though the potential for failure is higher, there is still the possibility for success to happen. Every single successful person you know has taken risks and had to jump – before you can start flying high, you need to jump high first. Before a bird learns to fly, the bird needs to jump out of the nest.

Pain is only temporary – while it may last for a minute, a day, or a year, eventually it will go – BUT you're better off regretting a mistake from taking a jump than regretting not jumping at all.

I'll tell you something that I wish I'd taken the jump in: my singing. Singing is my first love and when I had the opportunity to jump on a track, I got scared and said no. I kept thinking of the 'what ifs': what if I don't make it? What if I don't sound good? At the time I didn't have the mind-set I have now. Don't worry about the what ifs – they will only take you backwards when we are trying to get you forward.

You will get over the mistake, but you will never get over *not* taking the risk, because you will start thinking 'what if?' – and you will never be able to know because you never took the risk! If Michael Jordan didn't jump and shoot, there wouldn't be a Michael Jordan... I mean, he would still be there, but we wouldn't know about him.

Every single goal in your life should NOT be within arm's reach; it has to be somewhere out of your reach, somewhere where you need to stretch, swim, fly, jump, and fight to get it. If your goal doesn't challenge you, it will NOT change you. Success starts outside of your comfort zone, so GET OUT of your comfort zone.

Muhammad Ali once said that when he does push-ups and they start hurting his body, he starts counting from zero again because when his body aches, that's when the push-ups REALLY count. NO PAIN, NO GAIN.

REFLECTION TIME

When in your life are you scared to jump?
When in your life do you regret not taking risks?

TASK

Watch (on YOUTUBE): **Eric Thomas** – If you want to succeed.

What did you learn from this chapter? How has it helped you? Why don't you tell us on social media!

DON'T FORGET TO USE THE HASHTAG #ABC2S - @HayIsMulenda

K – KEEP CALM

Keep Calm – Not allowing nerves, fears, or worries to get the better of you.

"Every little thing is gonna be alright" – **Bob Marley.**

Now, once you jump in life, you're going to get worried, anxious, and nervous, but don't worry: KEEP CALM. One of the things I've learned in life is that everything works out in the end, and if it hasn't worked out, it's not yet the end. I said this in a previous chapter but it really is true. Many times we worry too much about certain things, but I have one question I'd like you to answer:

WHAT DO YOU GAIN FROM GETTING WORRIED?

A wise woman once said to me: *"worrying is like going outside with an umbrella on a sunny day, walking around with the umbrella up and expecting it to rain."* Worrying is looking at a situation and expecting something bad to happen, and guess what? Something bad probably *will* happen simply because you attracted it (the law of attraction).

You are a magnet and you attract certain situations from your actions, your energy, and your thoughts. If YOU want positive things to happen to you, you have to be positive, feel positive, and act positive. God will not give you what you want, but he will give you what you ARE. We are called human BEINGS for a reason, not human wantings. BE WHAT YOU WANT TO ATTRACT. If you want to attract good things, be good. If you want to attract worrying situations, be worried.

If you're sad, listening to a sad song will NOT help, as all the sad music will do is get you all up in your feelings. Instead, listen to the type of music you want your mood to be. If you want your mood to be happy, then listen to happy music, because it will automatically rub off onto your mood and influence it.

One motto I live by is 'Hakunna Matata', as alongside *Finding Dory* and *Finding Nemo*, *The Lion King* has to be one of my all-time favourite films. Now, let me just be honest and tell you that I'm not over Mufasa dying yet – Scar is such an idiot! But anyway, Hakunna Matata means 'no worries'. Remember back to chapter B? You're too blessed to be stressed, so make sure you always remember this. You gain nothing from being worried. A seed has to endure soil before it can grow, so if you're going through a situation right now, just understand that it's there to MAKE YOU AND BUILD YOU.

Sometimes you *do* need to break down before the breakthrough, and I myself had to go through that when I had my massive breakdown in early 2016. Mentally, I lost myself so I could find myself, and when you go through these kinds of struggles, you appreciate life more. Every test allows you to glorify the testimony. Bad things have to happen for you to REALLY appreciate the good, so just go with the flow because your good times are coming, and I know you will definitely appreciate them when they arrive.

I do have one pointer here as to how you should stop worrying. As many of us get in situations of worrying through assuming and not asking, please make sure that you ALWAYS ASK – assumption is the mother of frustration and it takes you nowhere. I won't lie; I used to assume EVERYTHING and it really affected me and made me overthink so much, but now I've let go of that mentality and it feels amazing! Try not to assume – no one gains anything. HONESTY IS THE BEST POLICY. ASKING IS KEY.

5 TIPS ON HOW TO KEEP CALM

- Prepare for the morning the night before.
- Avoid negative people.
- Write things down instead of trying to memorise them.
- Watch a video of a baby laughing.
- Don't bottle stuff up; talk to others.

RELECTION TIME

What can I do to stop myself from over-worrying?

What assumptions do I have in my life right now?

What can I do to keep more calm?

TASK

Create a 'keep calm' playlist – this will be a music playlist of calm music, happy music and positive music!

Music has such a huge impact on our emotions, and one of the best ways to keep calm is to actually listen to music!

What did you learn from this chapter? How has it helped you? Why don't you tell us on social media!

DON'T FORGET TO USE THE HASHTAG #ABC2SS - @HaylsMulenda

L – LOVE

I don't think love can be defined; personally, I feel it can only be felt.

"Love makes the world go round" – **Unknown.**

Keeping calm isn't always easy, but love will always have a big impact on your mood. If you surround yourself with people you love, do things you love, and love yourself, it will affect your mood and allow you to stay calm! Love is so beautiful – when you think of those you love, the food you love, the things you love... you just melt inside. I'm not talking just boyfriend-girlfriend love here; I'm talking about that real, real love: the love God has for us, the love a mother has for her child, the love a dog has for its owner... that DEEP, unconditional love.

You can't see love but you *can* feel it. You can't explain love but you *can* experience it. You see? Love is so important. Love can't be defined, only shown.

Now, there are three sections to this chapter:

1. **SELF-LOVE**

Self-love is the best type of love to have, simply because it's the most important. Through loving yourself, you are setting an example as to how others should love you, and through loving yourself, you are truly loving God because he created you in his image. I NEED you to understand that you are amazing, special, blessed, and beautiful/handsome, but before anyone else can see these things, you have to see them in yourself.

"No one can ever love you the way you love you" – **Fiona Makam-Pitoula.**

My best friend Fiona taught me how to love myself, and she also made me realise how important it is to always put yourself first, to love yourself first and to know yourself first. Before you are anyone else's, you are YOURS.

It's crazy, because sometimes we're so quick to tell others how we love them – and we will even go out of our way to show them our appreciation – but we often won't go out of our way to appreciate ourselves, or even love ourselves. Treating yourself by buying new trainers is not a sign of loving yourself; it's a sign of you loving those trainers.

By loving yourself you are realising your worth, your value, and your standard. Love yourself enough to walk away from anyone who's hurting you or from anything that's breaking you. And above all, love yourself enough to connect with God, because he really does love you.

It was only earlier this year that I learned to love myself, so for 18 years of my life I didn't even know what self-love was, but when I finally started the self-love journey, I never EVER turned back. Loving yourself is saying, "I know what's best for me, who is best for me, and why it's best for me," but make sure you don't get it twisted; there's a big difference between loving yourself and being plain damn selfish.

It's just like the thin line between confidence and cockiness – with self-love, you are loving yourself enough because you know your worth, and you are loving others because you know what true love feels like. Selfishness is putting yourself first and not caring who is affected by your actions or your words. Love yourself to know that you're special and that there's no one like you.

A FEW TIPS ON HOW TO LOVE YOURSELF

- Always put yourself first – never compromise your own happiness in order to make someone else happy. I did this for three years and it wasn't even worth it; I ended up getting hurt in the end. Cater to your happiness first before you cater to anyone else's.
- Constantly say good things about yourself, and always point out the beauty within you instead of the flaws – compliment yourself when looking in the mirror, and allow yourself to know that there's beauty inside of you.
- Stop listening to other people's opinions; they're not you.
- Read Psalms 139:14 and understand that God made you with purpose – you are fearfully and wonderfully made.
- Don't hang around with people who pull you down, upset you, or make you feel any less of a person. Know your worth and know when it's right to walk away from people who are of no benefit to you.

2. LOVING OTHERS

Treat others how you want to be treated – it's as simple as that. I know that others may treat you like crap but don't focus on this; focus only on how you treat others, because Karma is real and if you're not careful, Karma will slap you in the face.

We rise up by lifting others – we need to build bridges and not walls. This year (2016), many celebrities passed away and I remember someone saying to me, "Hayley, all the legends are dying!" I replied, "No they're not; we have legends in this generation but we're just not showing them the support and love they deserve".

If we showed others love the way we show these celebrities love, I'm pretty sure we would start to see legends forming in our own generation! People who are so quick to retweet and share a popular artist's music won't spend even one minute trying to retweet their friend's music – their OWN friend. Support your friends the same way you support these celebrities and maybe they'll be successful too. Life would be amazing if we supported others the way we want others to support us.

3. LOVING WHAT YOU DO

"Passion produces productivity" – **Hayley Mulenda.**

When you love what you do, you will commit so much more to it. Do what you love, love what you do. Have you ever heard the saying that if you do what you love, you will never work a day in your entire life? I definitely know how that feels. Ever since I started taking my speaking seriously and running my own business, I haven't felt like I've actually 'worked', even though this is my full time job – I love it so much, it just feels like a hobby that I get paid to do! They always say follow what you are made for, not what you are paid for, and it's true that the best teachers love what they do – you can see it in the way they teach! I had one teacher who loved teaching us, and because of that, we were all drawn to her. Loving what you do allows you to provide the best possible service in everything you do. After all, how can you serve when you're in a bad mood?

During my GCSE year, I remember being moved out of my RE set (I was in set four, the lowest set) and being placed into a special set with six other people. They told us that we were so bad at RE that they had to separate us from normal classes so we could be in a smaller, more intimate group. I hated RE so much! I didn't care about it and I didn't want to know, but that day I sat down and thought: 'wow, they've moved me to another set – I need to force myself to love RE'. They predicted me a C in that class for my GCSE but I forced myself to love it, I worked hard because I'd developed a passion, and this led to me getting my A. Passion produces productivity, and as I was passionate, I became far more productive.

REFLECTION TIME

Do you love yourself?

What can you do to show yourself more love?

What gestures can you do to show others around you that you love them?

What can you change about the things you hate in your life to make yourself passionate and productive?

TASK

Write yourself a love letter, telling yourself why you love yourself, complimenting yourself, and making yourself feel special. Put it away, then every time someone upsets you, read that letter and remember your worth.

What did you learn from this chapter? How has it helped you? Why don't you tell us on social media!

DON'T FORGET TO USE THE HASHTAG #ABC2SS - @HayIsMulenda

M – MINDSET

Mindset – The way you think, the way your mind and thoughts are set up.

"If you change the way you look at things, the things you look at change" – **Wayne Dyer.**

Love has an impact on how you feel, but your feelings first come from your thoughts, so it's very important to fill yourself not just with love but with positive thoughts as well. Your mind-set has a huge impact on both your results and your life, and you always have to try and look at the brighter side of life because there *is* a brighter side. Even the word 'Impossible' spells 'I'm Possible'. Your mind-set is everything, and life is all about perspective – there's the brighter side to life and the darker side to life, and it's up to you to choose which side you're on. The way you have problems is the same way you have blessings – the same way a cup could be half empty is the same way a cup could be half full.

You may not be where you want to be, but you're not where you used to be either! Having a positive mind-set is key, and as I've adopted this over the years, it is one thing that many people praise me for. I can honestly say it's changed my life; I am genuinely happier because I choose to have a better mind-set.

How your mind is set will determine how your life sets, so if you have an unproductive mind-set, it will lead you to do unproductive things – how? Well, your thoughts evoke your emotions, your emotions evoke your actions, and the outcomes in your life are based on those actions.

You gain nothing from being negative and you lose nothing from being positive – in fact, you gain peace from being positive! You will attract positive things in your life (the law of attraction) when you have a great mind-set, great people will want to be around you because great minds think alike. It's very important that you surround yourself with others who have a similar mind-set, because it'll have a big impact on yours. The great people I know all have great mind-sets – everything starts with your thoughts. What are you planting, weeds or seeds?

REFLECTION TIME

How is your mind-set?

How can you improve it?

TASK

Get a piece of paper and split it in two. On one side write 'negative' and on the other side write 'positive'.

On the negative side, put everything that's going wrong in your life, and on the positive side, mirror what you've written on the negative side but with an improved version of the same thing. So:

NEGATIVE – I AM BROKE.
POSITIVE – AT LEAST I HAVE ENOUGH MONEY TO BUY FOOD.

NEGATIVE – A CLOSE FRIEND HAS BETRAYED ME.
POSITIVE – AT LEAST I KNOW WHO MY CLOSE FRIENDS REALLY ARE.

After doing this, rip the paper in two. Throw away the negative side and hang up the positive side. There is always a good side to everything.

What did you learn from this chapter? How has it helped you? Why don't you tell us on social media!

DON'T FORGET TO USE THE HASHTAG #ABC2SS - @HaylsMulenda

N – NOW

Now – The Present, Today.

"You don't have to be great in order to get started but you need to start in order to be great" – **Les Brown.**

Unfortunately, many people wait until a certain time to start something: the new year, a new academic year, their birthday... the list goes on. CUT THIS OUT. This is such a bad habit, and just because it's a new year doesn't mean it's the only time there are going to be new opportunities – there are new opportunities every day! Why wait until a specific time in your life to claim them? CLAIM THEM NOW.

Today you were woken up, so today should be the day you make that change – today is your chance to get those new opportunities. The fact that you're seeing today at all shows that you still have purpose in your life, so don't waste it. No one is promised life today, so the fact that you're here shows how important your existence is – start working on your goals now, start working on your grades now; don't wait until a specific time for you to fix up.

Patience is a virtue, yes, BUT *"if opportunity does not knock on your door – BUILD ONE"* – **Milton Berle.**

That's right, sometimes waiting is necessary, but you can also start now, whilst you're waiting – let me show you how.

When a mother is pregnant she doesn't want to rush the pregnancy, because the baby takes nine months to develop properly and if she rushes the pregnancy, the baby could come out premature, leading to a higher risk of illness and health hazards. So, the mother has to be patient and wait for the full pregnancy so she can have a better chance of delivering a healthy baby. However, even though she has to wait nine months for the baby, she doesn't wait nine months to start buying clothes, equipment, nappies, and accessories – most mothers prepare beforehand and start building their nursery before the baby has even arrived!

So YES – be patient, but don't forget you can start your preparations RIGHT NOW! When you give birth to success, wouldn't you rather have been prepared for it?

REFLECTION TIME

What can you start doing today to impact your tomorrow?

What are you waiting for?

"Time flies when you're having fun" – What will you do to have fun so time flies? (Making sure it's something beneficial).

TASK

Make sure you plan your day, if you fail to plan, you're planning to fail. If you're able to point out exactly what you're going to do today, you'll be able to see what needs to be done tomorrow, and then it'll just be a domino effect until you reach success!

What did you learn from this chapter? How has it helped you? Why don't you tell us on social media!

DON'T FORGET TO USE THE HASHTAG #ABC2SS - @HaylsMulenda

O – OK STOP! EVALUATION TIME!

So, as we are roughly at the halfway point of this book, now is the best time to evaluate: evaluate in order to elevate.

This is where I need you to be completely honest, not with me but with yourself.

ARE YOU HAPPY WITH THE PROGRESS YOU'RE MAKING?

This is what I like to call the critical period. Life isn't just about what went well, life is all about the even better 'if'. There's always room for improvement, so now let's help you improve!

Before you move onto the next chapter – both in this book and in life – you need to be able to reflect on the last few chapters of your life. Now, this is the perfect time to look back over the book and over your life. You live and you learn; you grow from your experiences and from the information you gain. Knowledge comes through knowing, so know when to admit you're in the wrong and when you've made mistakes – that's the only way you can improve.

Now, it's time to evaluate your current position – get a notepad ready because it's time to break you down!

> A. Have you **accepted** your mistakes and accepted your current position in life? Do you know where you need to improve and elevate?

If no – remember that before you reach the finishing point, you need to have a starting point.

If yes – what areas of your life do you need to improve, and where exactly have you been going wrong and making mistakes?

Acceptance is the first step to success.

B. After every test there is a testimony, so what is your testimony? You have probably faced many trials and tribulations from which you've learned priceless lessons – so what have you learned? What were your **blessings**?

Remember, every lesson is a blessing.

C. In which areas are you **confident** about in your life? In which areas are you NOT confident in your life? Confidence will attract great things into your life.

D. What are you **determined** to accomplish by the end of this month (and if you're at the end of the month, then the end of next month)? Are your goals motivating? What are your goals and why?

You are destined for success, but before the destination comes the determination!

TOP TIP – WHAT IS A GOAL?

A DESIRED OUTCOME – SOMETHING YOU WANT TO ACCOMPLISH.

Your goals should always be **SMART:**

SPECIFIC – You need to know exactly what you want to accomplish, having a clear destination.

MEASURABLE – How will you know when you've reached your goal? Have a method where you'll be able to keep track that you're on the right path.

ATTAINTABLE – Be realistic with your goals. Can you actually accomplish them? Don't say you want to be diving in the Olympics tomorrow when you don't know how to swim.

RELEVANT – Do not set goals that are not relevant to you – this is not productive.

TIME – DEADLINE. Always have a deadline in mind as to when you want that goal to be completed!

E. Are you in the right **environment**? Are the people in your life helping you to grow? Are you watching productive programs? Listening to productive music? Going to productive events or seminars? Remember, you can still have fun whilst contributing to your growth.

   A flower can't grow with bleach and weeds.

F. Are you putting in the **Full Time Grind**? In which areas of your life do you need to make more commitment? Which areas need more focus?

   You reap what you sow.

G. How is your relationship with **God**? How do you expect someone to enter your house if you don't let them in? Let him IN and he will come (Jeremiah 29:13). Put God first in everything and he will put you first in everything too.

   Get God, Get Success.

H. How is your **health**? Your mental health? Your physical health?

What can you cut out in order to improve your health?

What mentally drains you? These things will need to be cut out, e.g. draining friends, bad music, bad food, and so on.

What physically drains you? These also need to be cut out e.g. certain foods and drinks.

Remember, your health is your wealth.

I. What type of **investments** are you making? Are these investments helping you to grow? Name three investments you will make in yourself this month in order to improve yourself, physically, mentally, and spiritually.

Investment means profit, so what are you gaining?

J. Have you **jumped**? Why are you scared to take risks? Where in your life do you *need* to take risks?

You must jump if you want to reach the next level.

K. Are you **keeping calm**? Is there anything you are worried about in your life? Why? How do you stop yourself from worrying? Praying? Reaching out to people?

Don't keep things in. After all, people are there to help and listen. Whether it's something big or small – always reach out and get things off your chest.

L. How can you show yourself more **love**? How can you show others more love? Who do you love unconditionally and why?

Why don't you randomly text someone you love telling them why you love them? Make them smile J

M. How is your **mind-set**? Is your mind-set positive? What are you feeding your mind with? What impacts on your mind-set the most? How can you improve it?

How your mind is set will determine how your year sets.

N. Are you starting **now**? Are you making serious power moves?

So what are you waiting for?! Lions chase their pray; they don't wait for it. Be a lion – go for it *now*.

P – PRODUCTIVE

Productive – Producing or being able to produce large amounts of goods, crops, and other commodities.

"The best way to predict the future is to create it" – **Alan Kay.**

Okay, now that we've evaluated your progress, we are able to make more productive steps to your success!

This part of the book relates back to 'Full Time,' where we talked about 'working hard' and 'working smart' – just because you're busy doesn't mean you're actually being productive, and being productive doesn't mean you have to be busy. Everyone can be busy, but not everyone can be productive. Remember what I said in Chapter F? Being busy could be a hamster running on a wheel; the hamster is constantly running on it, but everyone knows that wheel isn't going anywhere – it's just going round and round. Be careful and make sure that *your* wheel isn't just going round and round – you want your wheel to move forward, you want it to be productive!

Productivity relates to the rate and quality of your work, and it's a domino effect – what you're doing today will impact your tomorrow, but make sure you're not just being busy. You could be going to a seminar every single day, but is that seminar benefitting you? As I said, it's all about *growing* through life and not just *going* through life. Make sure that every single day you are contributing to your growth, and as productivity means to produce large amounts of goods, what goods are you producing in your life right now that are helping you reach the next level?

Arnold Schwarzenegger is an amazing actor, – just think of "I'll be back" - but some of you will also know that he started his journey in the Army. He initially wanted to be a bodybuilder – hence why he is so hench – so whilst he was in the Army he would use the regular training as his workout; he would wake up earlier than anyone else just so he could commit to his workout, and instead of just being 'busy' with his training, he was productive – he put in the extra hours and did the extra work so that he was able to become a successful bodybuilder, and in fact, he went on to do so much more! Being productive will take you higher than your original goal, so keep focused and be productive in everything you do.

REFLECTION TIME

Are you being productive? How? And if not, why not?

How can you increase your productivity?

TASK

Write down all the tasks you take part in on a day-to-day basis (swimming, revision, learning the piano, going out with friends, etc.) and tick the ones that are actually productive, so you're able to know the difference.

What did you learn from this chapter? How has it helped you? Why don't you tell us on social media!

DON'T FORGET TO USE THE HASHTAG #ABC2SS - @HayIsMulenda

Q – QUIT QUITTING

Quitting – Not finishing what you have started.

"Pain is temporary, Quitting is forever" **– Eric Thomas**.

The best way to be productive is purely by not quitting, as productivity involves consistency! This chapter is going to be quite short, simply because it speaks for itself.

If you spend the same amount of time focusing on winning rather than on doubting yourself, then trust me when I say you will definitely be successful. You are born with purpose and that purpose is to win – after all, the first race you were ever in, you WON (in the race of the sperm, your sperm won), and the fact that you won the first race you'd ever participated in just goes to show you are a winner.

If Michael Jordan had quit when he didn't make his high school basketball team, would he be the greatest athlete in the world? No.

If Muhammad Ali had quit once he lost his first fight, would he still be one of the greatest? No.

If Coca-Cola quit after selling only 25 bottles of drink in their first year, would it still be the world's leading soft drink company? No.

Don't quit. DO IT.

I also have a story to illustrate just how important it is that you don't quit. It was the 14th of August 2015, and I had just received my A-Level results. I didn't get the grades I wanted, and for this reason I ended up having to go through clearing. Now, clearing is a very daunting, frustrating, and scary place to be. Basically, YOU HAVE NO CHOSEN UNIVERSITY AND YOU'RE NOT IN CONTROL OF ANYTHING. I was so anxious, though praying helped – the fact that I didn't quit praying and that I didn't quit trying to find a university is what led me to being accepted into a better university than the university that had ORIGINALLY DECLINED ME.

If you DON'T STOP, your blessings won't stop EITHER! If you don't succeed, try, try, and try again. You are better off failing from trying than dying and regretting the fact that you didn't try at all.

Les Brown is one of my favourite motivational speakers, and the reason why I love him so much is because of the fact that he is *real*; there's no sugar-coating with him at all. He will simply TELL you how it is and he is just so real. He told the following story, and upon hearing this story, my life changed that very same day:

There was a man who was on his deathbed, and as he lay there, many ghosts appeared and surrounded him. The ghosts were very angry, and this man was very scared, so he asked them, "Who are you and why are you angry?" The ghosts replied, "We are the ghosts of your unused talents, skills, and ideas!" and the man said, "Okay, but why are you angry? What do you want from me?" To this the ghosts replied, "Every single one of us wanted to be shown to the world, but now we can't and we're angry because the world will never see us. You gave up on us and now... now we have to die with you." At those words the man started to cry very hard, and it was at that moment that he started to regret. He saw all these talents, ideas, and skills inside of him, but because he gave up, those ghosts had to disappear with him.

Now my question to you is: how many ghosts will die with you on your deathbed?

The richest place is the graveyard; don't take your million pound ideas, skills, and talents with you to that place.

REFLECTION TIME

What have you given up on? And why?

Name three things you don't want to give up, and think about how you'll make *sure* you don't give up.

TASK

Write a contract saying: 'I **'insert name here'** have agreed not to give up and to keep on going.' Then, insert all of the reasons as to why you shouldn't give up, and sign it at the bottom. Now, every time you feel like giving up, go back to that contract you made and read it through again – after all, contracts should never be broken!

What did you learn from this chapter? How has it helped you? Why don't you tell us on social media!

DON'T FORGET TO USE THE HASHTAG #ABC2SS - @HaylsMulenda

R – RACE

Race – To move or progress swiftly.

"The only person you are racing is you, so you've got this!" –
Hayley Mulenda.

Run a race to win, not to quit!

We are all trying to race to the finish line, which is fine, but you need to remember that you can take your time – you're not racing anyone but yourself. Everyone is running their own race at their own pace, so please don't compare your race to anyone else's; if you keep looking left and right, focusing on others whilst you're meant to be running, you will end up getting distracted before you get anywhere near that finish line.

WINNERS FOCUS ON WINNING AND LOSERS FOCUS ON WINNERS. Focus on the finishing line, not the others.

Unfortunately, social media has put us in a place where it has now become the norm to compare our lives to others on a daily basis, but let me tell you something – no one has your story and no one has walked your path but you. Therefore, comparison of any kind is pointless.

You need to embrace the fact that your journey is one of a kind – there is NO 'we' in *vision*, ONLY 'I'. You shouldn't expect everyone to understand your vision, journey, or race; that is between you and God alone. Personally, I don't expect anyone to understand what I'm doing or why I'm doing it, because God has given me my own vision and not someone else's.

One book I highly recommend is **The Alchemist by Paul Coelho** – this book has taught me so much in regards to the journey of life, and it has also taught me that we are all running our own race, and while we won't always be going at the pace we want to be, that doesn't matter, because it's not about how fast you're moving; all that matters is that you *are* moving. On our journey we are going to encounter setbacks, distractions, and all sorts, but if we keep focused on the finish line and not on the distractions, we will get there slowly but SURELY.

You will not win immediately but definitely – and that's all that matters.

REFLECTION TIME

What pace are you running at? Fast? Slow? Medium?

Are you happy with your pace?

What can you do to stop comparing your race to someone else's?

TASKS

Write down all the things you have rushed and all the things you don't want to rush!

What did you learn from this chapter? How has it helped you? Why don't you tell us on social media!

DON'T FORGET TO USE THE HASHTAG #ABC2SS - @HaylsMulenda

S – SETBACK

Setback – Facing a circumstance that may affect you in a negative way.

"A slingshot has to be pulled back in order for it to propel forward" – **Hayley Mulenda.**

Losing isn't running a race and falling down; losing is falling down, and refusing to get up again and carry on running!

In life we all go through setbacks; not everything is going to go our way, and that's okay! Let's deny that life is perfect, and if there's one thing we all have in common it's that we all have experience with setbacks, trials, tests, and pain. However, before the testimony comes the test, and before the breakthrough comes the breakdown – a flower cannot grow until the seed has endured soil, and therefore before you can grow you're going to have to be buried. Before a diamond is formed it has to be put under pressure, so you see, setbacks are not only inevitable but NECESSARY too.

A setback is just a setup for a COMEBACK. Sometimes we need the bad results to fix up, and you never appreciate the light until you've experienced darkness. If you feel you are having a setback right now – you're NOT. You're simply learning.

Life is a learning process: you live and you learn. In every test you learn a lesson, every test is there to challenge you, and in every challenge you improve. As you grow so will your battles, so will your trials. The higher your trees grow towards the heavens, the deeper your roots grow towards hell, simply because you need the balance – bigger tests mean bigger testimonies. God will never allow a weak soldier to go through a strong battle; God would never put you in a situation that you can't handle, because during every bad situation you've been in God has pulled you through, and if he hasn't pulled you through yet, he is PULLING you through right now.

My best friend Javen is a great example of turning a setback into a comeback. Javen failed year 12 – he left sixth form with 2 Us and a C. The grades Javen got were his setback, but then he realised it was best to move to another sixth form away from all his friends so he could focus and re-sit the year. And that's exactly what he did: Javen ended up re-sitting the whole year – him failing only motivated him to work even harder. After being pulled back, Javen propelled himself into the best university for his course in the UK. He was set back, he failed year 12 but he set up, he acknowledged his mistakes, moved to another 6th form then fixed up by working 10x harder and he came back, this time bigger and better.

REFLECTION TIME

With every setback, you always need to assess it!

What setbacks are you facing right now?

How did you get there?

What can you learn from this test?

TASK

Get a piece of paper, split it into two, and on one side write 'setbacks' and on the other side write 'comebacks'. On the setbacks side write down all the setbacks you've ever had and on the comebacks side write down how you're going to recover from that setback and what your comeback is.

What did you learn from this chapter? How has it helped you? Why don't you tell us on social media!

DON'T FORGET TO USE THE HASHTAG #ABC2SS - @HaylsMulenda

T – TIME

Time – A commodity that can never come back, it is measured in minutes, hours, and days.

"The trouble is you think you have time" – **Buddha.**

If you focus on a setback for too long, you will end up losing time, and time isn't something to be wasted! Time is so precious – in fact, it's the most precious thing you have. Your time is your life, and without time there is no life, LITERALLY.

Time is the only commodity you will never get back. You can always spend 100 pounds and get it back at some point, but you can't spend 100 minutes and get *that* back. Ever. If we valued time the way we value money, life would be so different.

Often we waste time, which is incredibly dangerous – time isn't something to be wasted. You have to ask yourself: where exactly is my time going? Is where I'm spending my time helping me grow? Is it benefiting me? Is it helping others?

A lot of people say that they wish they had more time, but they're waking up at 1pm. The early bird catches the worm! Try and wake up earlier; the more hours you allow yourself to have, the more productive you are likely to be.

When I started waking up earlier, I started to do way more within one day than ever before, which allowed me to feel like I'd used my time wisely. As I said, the worst thing you can do is waste time, simply because you'll never get it back.

Now, I have a question for you: if you woke up every single day with a clock by your bed, counting down how much time you had left in life, *would you live your life differently?* Yes? Then you need to live your life differently *now*, because you don't know how much time you have left. Today is the youngest you will ever be. Now, this moment, this very second – YOU WILL NEVER GET IT BACK.

We waste time so easily and we don't even realise it. 1/3 of our lives is spent on sleep, so what exactly are you doing with the other 2/3? Are you spending that time wisely, using it to elevate? To grow? To reach your goals? And if not, why not?

Wasting time is like wasting your life. Value time because you are actually valuing life. Every single day, God deposits 24 hours into your bank account – that's his gift to you, but how you use those 24 hours is your gift back to him.

So, what gift are you giving back to God?

REFLECTION TIME

Where do you need to stop wasting time?

What will you do in order to be more productive with your time?

TASK

Outline where your time goes and figure out what you need to commit less time to.

E.g. 30% sleep.
40% studying.
30% games.

What did you learn from this chapter? How has it helped you?
Why don't you tell us on social media!

DON'T FORGET TO USE THE HASHTAG #ABC2SS - @HaylsMulenda

U – UNIQUE

Unique – Being one of a kind, unlike anyone else.

"The greatness of art is not to find what is common but what is unique" – **Isaac Singer.**

God spent time creating you, and he took his time because you are unique! Yes, you have a super power, and that super power is that there is no one else like you, anywhere. There are seven billion people in the world but only ONE you, and if you being unique isn't important enough, then I don't know what else is.

God made you for you. He could have chosen for all of us to be completely the same, but he didn't: he made us with different colours, different hair textures, different DNA, different eyes, different feet, different toe nails… DIFFERENT EVERYTHING. Of course, some things may be similar, but nothing is actually the *same*.

Be yourself. Why? Because everyone else is already taken. You have been created for your own purpose, your own vision, and your own dreams – if you don't build on your own dreams, you will end up helping someone else build theirs! Embrace your uniqueness, because if everyone else is wearing black and white, wouldn't you want to be wearing colours? By embracing your uniqueness, this is what exactly happens – you STAND OUT.

You need to embrace who you are, because if you don't, no one else will.

Act Like A Success, Think Like A Success by Steve Harvey, has taught me that if you want to improve things around you, you first have to improve things that are *in* you. Work on yourself and everything else will follow, so work on your talent and your skills, then the opportunities will come to you. The best companies/people focus on the innovation rather than the product – innovation means making changes to something established, and these changes are done to improve what is already established. Work on yourself, and make changes to enhance your uniqueness.

Steve Harvey talks about finding your gift and then using it to your advantage. When you are able to find out what's unique about you – what you're good at – and use it to your advantage, YOU ARE UNSTOPPABLE.

Earlier on I briefly talked about innovation, and I also talked about how this book is an innovative book because I've taken a concept that everyone knows – the alphabet – and presented it in a new way. Steve Jobs is an amazing example of innovation. He took the concept of music and phones to a new level, focusing on making Apple so unique that when they told him to go away, a few years later they begged him to come back – why? Because he was unique. Simply put, no one could do it like Steve Jobs. At first people may not like you because they don't understand you, but don't worry – they'll soon be running after you.

There's no harm in being different, so claim your uniqueness and use it to your advantage. Personally, I felt that as a young black girl I should have so many barriers stopping me from what I want to achieve, however, I always say, "Use the minority to get the majority".

Growing up I always thought that my age, gender, and ethnicity could limit me from doing what I wanted to do, that was until I got to a certain age and realised that, in fact, being a minority is THE BEST THING EVER.

We all are minorities in our own way, whether it be due to age, race, sexuality, location, or religion... we all have a barrier that limits our options, and one thing I hate is the fact the media will never tell you that being a minority is important – the fact that you are a minority should even be your WHY; it should be the reason why you shouldn't stop pursuing anything you want to in life. Why should the fact that I am black, young, and female limit me from the dream of being successful? The whole advantage of being a minority is the fact that you're UNIQUE. You're one of the few who SHOULD do it, COULD do it, and WILL do it.

Barack Obama is an amazing example, and let's not lie here and say he wasn't just favoured for his political campaign; his likeliness came from his ethnic background. One thing I always get told is, *"You've achieved so much for your age!"* Do you see what I mean? Being a minority is actually an advantage; people will always praise you 10 times more for being one of a kind.

For all the people who've been told you can't do something because of who you are, DO IT ANYWAY, BECAUSE YOU WILL STAND OUT. Many people lined up to watch the red moon, but why? It's only a moon. No – It's a red moon. Many people will line up to push your success, but why? It's only a human. No – It's because you're unique.

REFLECTION TIME

What is unique about you?
How will this make you stand out?
How will you use your minority to get the majority?

TASK

Make a list of everything that is unique about you and then write down how each gift can help you stand out from the crowd.

What did you learn from this chapter? How has it helped you? Why don't you tell us on social media!

DON'T FORGET TO USE THE HASHTAG #ABC2SS - @HaylsMulenda

V – VICTOR NOT VICTIM

Victim – A person who has come to feel helpless and passive by the face of misfortune, allowing it to overcome them.

Victor – a person who defeats an enemy or circumstance t in a battle.

"Use your circumstances to empower you, not overpower you"
– **Hayley Mulenda.**

God didn't just make you unique, but also a victor!

The one thing we forget as humans is that everyone is fighting their own battle – and even you are. Sometimes we forget that we are bigger than every obstacle thrown at us, so just remember this: fear is FALSE EVIDENCE APPEARING REAL. Your obstacles may seem bigger than what they are, but don't be a victim, BE A VICTOR.

Don't make excuses; make results. Now, I am a very honest person, so let me just be honest with you here – people don't care about what you have been through; they care about what you have overcome.

Life will only overtake you if you allow it to – trust me. At the age of 15, I nearly got stabbed, and on that day I thought I was going to lose my life. My mind was racing with all type of thoughts, and this experience led to me being anxious, scared to leave my house, and hating myself. However, through having faith and hope that I would overcome it, I did! And now that I *have* overcome it, I've been able to inspire others to overcome their own issues. Life certainly isn't easy, but like I said, nothing good in life comes easy: to get good grades you have to put in the hard work, and to get a good body you have to work out. This stuff comes with tears, sweat, and sometimes even blood (though I hope not!).

One week before my AS sociology exam, I received a letter in the post from my sociology teacher, saying that he felt I was going to get a D and that I wasn't doing at all well in the subject. This annoyed me so much, BUT I didn't let this overpower me – instead, I allowed it to EMPOWER ME. After receiving that letter, I revised harder than ever before and ended up getting an A. By going from being predicted a D to getting an A, I showed them I was victor, **NOT victim**.

Whilst we're on this topic, I want to highlight one thing that people like to be a victim of: their PAST.

Now, you are *not* a victim of your past unless you *allow* yourself to be. You are greater than your past, so don't let others – or even yourself – use your past against you. If anyone *does* want to use your own past against you, that says more about them than it does about you. Don't let a judgement become your reality. Everyone has a past, and who are you to bring up someone else's? Use your past to elevate you NOT devastate you. Your past is your past for a reason – do not stay there. LIFE IS IN THE PRESENT.

You have a story, but don't allow your story to overpower you; instead, use that story to empower you and others around you.

REFLECTION TIME

What have you overcome?
What are you still battling? What can you do to overcome it?

TASK

Write a letter to your younger self (say, five years ago), talking about how far you have come. Talk about what you have accomplished, and highlight what you have overcome, giving your younger self some advice about overcoming situations.

Then, every time you feel discouraged, read that letter and remember you were born a VICTOR.

What did you learn from this chapter? How has it helped you? Why don't you tell us on social media!

DON'T FORGET TO USE THE HASHTAG #ABC2SS - @HayIsMulenda

W – WHY

Why – The reason as to why you want to be successful.

"When you feel like quitting, remember WHY you started"
– Unknown.

Everything you have overcome in your life is a reason as to *why* you should want to be successful; you will be successful because what's inside you is far more powerful than any obstacle that can ever be thrown at you.

Now we're getting to the last few chapters of the book, and you're probably thinking there's been a lot of knowledge but not enough motivation. Well, this chapter right here is where the motivation goes deep; this chapter will be enough to motivate you to get you where you need to go. This is where I will also share with you what motivates me personally.

In the last chapter we talked about battles, and while we all want to be successful and get somewhere in life, most of the time we lack the motivation to do it. Fortunately, I know just how to change that – YOUR WHY.

WHAT'S YOUR WHY?

Why do you want to be successful? And who are you doing it for? Some of you have lost parents, some of you have lost siblings, and some of you don't even have parents. THAT'S WHY YOU NEED TO PUSH HARD.

My mother gets on her knees every single night – regardless of how tired she is – and prays to God, hoping that he will bless me and allow me to be successful. I know I can't waste my mum's prayers – THAT'S WHY I HAVE TO PUSH HARD.

At three years of age I lost my dad, so I never grew up with a father figure, but I *do* know it hasn't been easy growing up in a single parent household. Me, my mum, and my brother have gone through a lot, and as I was growing up, I decided that I didn't want my mum to go through it any longer – THAT'S WHY I PUSH SO HARD.

My dad's gone, but when I meet him again, the first thing I want to hear from him are the words, "I am proud of you, Hayley" – that's why I go so hard.

As I mentioned before, in early 2016 I got into a really bad place and I even became suicidal. I went through so much in such a short period of time that I couldn't cope, my mum couldn't cope, and neither could my brother or my friends. I was in and out of hospital and I was going through a very, very bad break-up as well – this literally broke me. However, I remember that whilst sitting on my bed in the dark, I prayed to God, saying, "if you are able to get me out of this dark place, I promise that I will push HARDER than ever." God answered my prayers – he took me out of that place and I go HARDER than ever to say thank you to him; I don't want to waste God's blessing. In year 7/8 I was bullied, an experience that left me feeling incredibly lonely, but this actually pushed me to be the loving person I am today – I never want anyone to feel lonely like I did, so if I can do anything to change that for someone, I will. I've had exes, old friends, and even family members betray me, and because people like that are waiting for me to fail – I just make sure I keep them waiting!

Once I was set up by a 'friend' of mine, leaving me in a situation that led to me nearly being stabbed and being robbed of £150, and in 2014 (I remember this like it was yesterday) I got a call from my brother telling me that my mother had been admitted to hospital. I rushed from sixth form to go visit my mum, and as I saw her lying on a hospital bed – after being diagnosed with her medical condition – I realised that my mum wasn't getting any younger, so what was I going to do to make sure she lived the rest of her life comfortably? My mum is my world, and THAT IS WHY I have to be successful and make my mum proud; she's been through TOO much for me to just sit back and be lazy.

I first started motivational speaking at the age of 17 and I registered my company when I was 18. I had loved ones laugh in my face, telling me I was too young and that I wouldn't be successful, and I even had teachers telling me I wouldn't be successful with it … Well, here I am now at 19 with my first ever book – the best way to get someone back (by far) is by silencing them with your success!

I used EVERYTHING that was working against me to work *for* me. I used THIS as my why.

Do you have people who have left you? **That's your why.**
People who have died? **That's your why.**
People who have betrayed you? **That's your why.**
Do you want to make someone proud? **That's your why.**

Some of you have been through some deep, deep stuff, and you DESERVE a better life, which is why you should work hard to get it. YOU are destined for greatness, and you *will* get there if you just remember your why.

REFLECTION TIME

What's your why?

What did you learn from this chapter? How has it helped you? Why don't you tell us on social media!

DON'T FORGET TO USE THE HASHTAG #ABC2SS - @HaylsMulenda

X – X RAY TIME

So, in **Chapter O**, we did the first set of evaluations – now, this is PART 2.

It's time to evaluate and elevate, and for this we are going to x-ray you. We need to break you down before we can build you up.

So, ask yourself: What have you learned so far? And how are you implementing this book into your life? Before we move onto the last two chapters, we need to summarise the previous ones, so now it's time to **grab your pen and notepad!**

> P. Are you being *productive*? What areas of your life would you say are the most productive? What areas of your life would you say are the least productive?
>
> Remember that being productive – and not just being 'busy' – is what will get you to the next level.

> Q. What pushes you to *quit*? Name one thing you don't want to give up and why.
>
> DON'T QUIT, DO IT.

> R. Are you happy with the *race* you're running? Are you happy with the pace you're running at? Are you

happy with the people you are racing with? Who are you running your race for? For yourself? Or for others?

Remember not to compare your race to someone else's; even if you see someone reach the finish line before you, it doesn't matter – that's *their* finish line and NOT yours.

A dog gives birth in a few months to dozens of small puppies, but an elephant gives birth in 24 months to a huge elephant – look at yourself as the elephant; your big blessing will come through, so don't worry if you see others getting their small mini blessings before you.

S. What **setbacks** have you experienced? What lessons have you learned from those setbacks? And how are you setting up for the comeback?

Every setback is a setup for a comeback.

T. Where is your **time** going? Who are you spending the most time with? What are you spending the most time on? And how do you think you can manage your time better?

Don't forget that time is the most precious thing in the world – no time means no life.

U. What is **unique** about you? What do you have that no one else has? What's your minority and how will you use this minority to get the majority?

There's a U in success and a U in unique.

V. What have you overcome to be the **victor**? What are you battling right now? And how will you overcome that battle?

God will never allow you to battle something you can't overcome.

Now that we've finished this evaluation, think carefully about how you've answered these questions, and then make sure you implement them into your life!

Y – YOUTH

Youth – The days when you're young, wild, and free!

"Don't waste your youth growing up" – **Pablo Picasso.**

A beautiful woman once said (Whitney Houston) "I believe the children are the future, teach them well and LET THEM lead the way." This book was initially aimed for young people – me being young myself, I get it. I understand. I get the whole, "I want to live my life" thing, but I'm telling you that the whole partying, having fun, and the motives – they will ALWAYS be there, but you will *never* be this age again. Remember when I said this is the youngest you will ever be? Well, it's true.

The one thing I love about being young is the fact that you're allowed to take risks, you're allowed to mess up, to find yourself, to work on yourself, and to live life! This is actually the best time to live life, because your youth are the days that go quickly, but they are always the days that are best remembered.

My friend Abraham Adams has been one person who has taught me how important it is to take risks at a young age, because between the ages 18-25 we are able to make mistakes and bounce right back. Why? Because we have so much life ahead of us!

I never want to get to 70 years old and say to myself, "I wish I'd done this at 19," or "I wish I'd done this at 20." NO. I AM 19 NOW SO I AM GOING TO DO IT. Many people wait until a certain age to try. *No*, try now – you have nothing to lose! You have age on your side, time on your side, health on your side, and energy on your side; you won't be as active when you grow older, so do things *now*!

I look at my seven-year-old cousin and think 'HOW DO YOU HAVE SO MUCH ENERGY?' You never want to go through life and stay in the same place because of fear or because of others, and if you just follow what everyone else is doing, you'll end up exactly like everyone else.

In my first year of university, instead of clubbing and going out, I stayed in, creating business plans, planning motivational talks, recording motivational videos, and studying. I had people tell me I was boring and that I was wasting my youth, but everyone kept quiet once they saw me winning three awards, being featured in *The Huffington Post* and international articles in America and Austria, being in newspapers, conducting two talks at the houses of parliament, talking to thousands of young people across the UK, getting booked in another country, and having my first book published all before the age of 19! One thing people always comment on is my work rate, and the fact that I am young is one reason why I work so hard. I've had to sacrifice so much but it's been totally worth it. The fact that I am young is the *reason* why people want to book me, the *reason* why young people want to listen to me – so remember: USE YOUR MINORITY TO GET THE MAJORITY. WORK NOW AND PLAY LATER.

When it comes to you wanting to achieve goals and grind hard, you should start young. Why? Because the world is your oyster. You have time on your side, more energy, no commitment, you're probably still living at home meaning no rent, you're probably not married, and you probably don't have any kids – this allows you to focus on you and you alone.

How to Be a Student Entrepreneur by **Junior Ogunyemi** was the book that taught me the benefits of being young, and it's true that in life people are trying so hard to grow up, but that shouldn't be the case – you should just go with the flow. If you try to grow up too quickly, you end up dealing with grown-up situations at such a young age, and why put yourself through that stress just because you want to feel older?

REFLECTION TIME

Is age stopping you from achieving what you want?

How can you use your age as an advantage to do what you need to do?

TASK

Write down a list of things you want to do before a certain age, and then go and DO IT! (E.g. skydiving, swimming with dolphins, etc. etc.)

What did you learn from this chapter? How has it helped you? Why don't you tell us on social media!

DON'T FORGET TO USE THE HASHTAG #ABC2SS - @HayIsMulenda

Z – ZEAL

Zeal – Great energy or enthusiasm for a cause

"Zeal will do more than knowledge" – **William Hazlitt.**

Your youth is full of ZEAL, so don't waste it – you have SO much energy!

Now we've reached the last chapter, and you probably have a rough idea as to what areas need tweaking whilst travelling on your success journey – I always say that success is a journey and not a destination, and this book is here to ensure that you are on the right journey. You have now learned different techniques, lessons, and steps, but none of that can actually be of any use unless you *put* it to use. It's all about the energy that YOU are putting in.

TO GET 100 YOU NEED TO GIVE 100.

Always put in your everything, your all, as what you put in is exactly what you get out – we've talked about committing your time, but committing your energy is JUST as important.

You are your own fuel; you can never rely on anyone or anything else to give you energy. Energy cannot be found, nor can it be created; energy is always there, you just need to use it! Regardless of whether you're getting paid or not, or whether you're benefitting or not benefitting – always put your all into it!

If you ever EVER run out of energy, ALWAYS remember YOUR WHY.

Now, I have a story of a builder and a king to illustrate why it's so important to *always* give your all.

There was a builder who had been building for over 50 years, and just one day before his retirement, he sat in his small house, thinking about life and getting excited about retiring. He couldn't WAIT to retire and maybe move into a bigger house, but whilst the man was planning his life after retirement, his holidays, and upgrading his house, he got a call from the king, asking him to build just one more house in the countryside – he said he would cover all the costs, stating that this house was important and that he could use any materials he wanted, and any furniture he wanted, no matter how expensive. The king also reinforced the fact that a gift would be given to him to say thank you for his 50 years of work.

Now, the builder was very angry, simply because he wanted to retire the next day and now he couldn't because he had to build the house that the king wanted, so the builder told himself he would use cheap materials, rush it, and put in no effort so that he would be able to retire quicker. And that's exactly what he did: he was able to build the house in just two days, but it was disgusting, poor, cheap, and in bad condition. The excited builder then called the king after building the house in the countryside, stating that he'd finished and asking what his gift would be. Well, the king replied, "I know you are the best builder in the country and I know this house you built for me is amazing, so your gift is that house: I have removed all of your items out of your old house and given you this one – I knew that because I was covering the costs you would use the best material, get the best furniture, and put proper effort and energy into it, so thank you for your work! Have fun in your new house."

The builder put in energy for 50 years, and just because he didn't give his all once, he lost his house – are you willing to lose it all just because you wanted to rush things and put in no energy?

REFLECTION TIME

Do you always give it your all?
Where do you need to put in more effort?

TASK

Get yourself a folder and put together all of your notes, reflection points, and tasks so that you're able to reflect and implement this alphabet into your life on a daily basis!

What did you learn from this chapter? How has it helped you? Why don't you tell us on social media!

DON'T FORGET TO USE THE HASHTAG #ABC2SS - @HaylsMulenda

MY LETTER TO YOU

I thought that since we've been going through the alphabet letters, I should write a letter to you.

Dear Reader,

If you're reading this it's either because you've skipped through the alphabet (which is wrong, so GO BACK AND FINISH THE BOOK), or because you have actually completed this book from chapters A-Z. I just want you to know that I am so, so proud of you. You have taken the time out of your day to reflect, improve, and elevate. You have taken the time to do tasks, ask yourself questions, and be true to yourself. Not only have you *accepted* your current position, counted all your *blessings,* and enhanced your *confidence,* but you have been *determined* to finish what you started! WHICH IS THIS BOOK. Not only have you placed yourself in a better *environment,* and committed *full time* to your goals, but you have allowed *God* to be in the centre of it. You have improved your *health, invested* in yourself, and *jumped* so you were able to fly. I know that through this book you were able to *keep calm,* which allowed you to *love* the journey to success, change your *mindset,* and start fixing up *NOW!*

Okay, you have been through the evaluation process – and I know it's allowed you to be more *productive* – so now you're on your way. Don't *quit.* Run your *race* and don't allow any *setbacks* to get in your way. Use your *time* wisely, remember you are *unique,* and be the *victor* in every circumstance. Remember who you're doing it for and *why* you started, *x-ray* yourself daily, and don't forget that you're still *young,* so the world is your oyster. Finally, make sure you have the *zeal* to finish big and win big!

You are destined for greatness and I can't wait to hear all of your testimonies and success stories. You have disciplined yourself to finish what you started, and don't forget, discipline is key: discipline allows you to focus, and if you focus on the goal, you will *always* reach it. If you don't shower every day, you start to stink, so if you don't motivate yourself every day, life will start to stink! Motivation is needed daily so don't feel that you won't have to re-read this book now that you've finished it! Use this book whenever you need a reminder. It is here with you for life, and hopefully it'll be passed on to your kids and your kids' kids – why not teach them the alphabet a little differently as well?

You are now equipped with the ABCs to student success, and I can't wait to see you at the top! One thing I do want you to understand is that you will make mistakes, but that's fine – you're human, and it's okay to make mistakes. Not everything works out the first time, but the whole concept of life is to live and learn. You also need to realise that not everything will go the way you want it to, but just remember that God's plan is greater than your plan. Trust in him and seek him for guidance.

May God bless you, guide you, and be with you in everything you do and everywhere you go.

Once you've finished reading this page, please email me so I can send you a gift for officially starting the journey to student success!

EMAIL: INFO@HAYLEYMULENDA.COM
SUBJECT: ON MY WAY TO STUDENT SUCCESS

In your email, please include the following:

- How has this book been of benefit to you?
- Has your perception on life changed after reading this book?
- If you could sum up this book in just one word, what would it be?

Of course, please feel free to include any other comments or anything else you'd like to say!

I look forward to hearing from you!

Don't forget to tell a friend! Why not buy them this book? Or perhaps recommend it to them? Let's share this alphabet around! Let's teach the alphabet in a new way! And don't forget to leave a review on Amazon – thank you!

Blessings,
Hayley Mulenda

MEET HAYLEY

IMAGINEREEL PRODUCTIONS

"I'm on a mission to motivate and inspire every young person, to help them understand their dreams can become reality."

My Name is Hayley Mulenda and I see myself as an altruistic character; I gain satisfaction from helping others.

Altruism is the opposite of egoism, it's the concern of others and gaining happiness from caring about other peoples needs.

An aspiration of mine is to help someone else conquer their own aspirations. I believe that success starts within; you are already capable of reaching success in whatever field you want to conquer.

I'M HERE TO HELP YOU BELIEVE IT!

ISAAC NOMUAH

Hayley Mulenda is a Multi-Award Winning Youth Motivational Speaker and Entrepreneur who aspires to help others reach their aspirations! She is described as 'the spark': the spark to hope, the spark to inspiration, and the spark that is needed to help you get out of bed at 7am in the morning. Positive For Youth admires her as an individual for the fact that at such a young age she managed to build her own registered motivational speaking company, promoting education to school children all over the UK. 'I am on a mission to motivate and inspire you to help YOU reach your dreams.' Over the past few years, Hayley has talked to thousands of students across the UK, sharing stages with Action Jackson, Alim Kamara, Lord Popat, Suli Breaks, and many more!

The Huffington Post has recognised Hayley as an incredible young woman who is doing inspirational work in the world!

AWARDS

- **BE (Black Enterprise) Mogul - Most Influential and Most Inspirational Black Entrepreneur in Britain for Under 21** *Supported by NatWest, 10 Downing Street and Mayor of London* - 2016
- **Positive for Youth Inspire Award Winner** - *2015*
- **Jack Petchey Achievement Award Winner** - *2015*
- **People of The Year (YOPEY) Nominee** - *2015*
- **National Diversity Award Nominee** - *2015/2016*
- **BEAM Awards 'Inspiration of The Year' Nominee** -*2016*

Hayley has toured up and down the UK, working with different universities (including Russell group) and talking to thousands of students in different secondary schools, colleges, and youth organisations. Her talks and seminars have been described as 'life-changing', 'inspirational', and 'fun' and she herself has been described as a force not to be reckoned with and a young person to look out for in the future. People of her generation adore her and class her as nothing but inspiring, and by integrating love, wisdom, and humour, she's able to empower young people in a way they'll never forget! She likes to consider herself an ordinary young person who just wants to succeed in life and wants to help others do the same.

HAYLEY MULENDA IS MOTIVATED TO MOTIVATE YOU!

DARNELL DEPRADINE

REFERENCES

Coelho, Paulo. *The Alchemist*. New York, N.Y.: HarperCollins, 1998. Print.

Harvey, Steve and Jeffrey Johnson. *Act Like A Success, Think Like A Success*. Print.

Ogunyemi, Jackson. *Shut Up & Take Action: The No Nonsense Guide To Success And Happiness*. 2013. Print.

Ogunyemi, Junior. *How To Be A Student Entrepreneur*. St Albans, Herts, Scotland: Ecademy Press, 2011. Print.

Printed in Germany
by Amazon Distribution
GmbH, Leipzig